LEARN ABOUT

Identity

Who are you?
2

What are you like?
4

What do you like?
6

What do you need?
8

How do you learn best?
10

How do you cope with difficulties?
12

How do you feel about your looks?
14

What makes a person attractive, after all?
16

Do you and your parents listen to one another?
18

Do you feel valued and accepted?
20

What makes you unique?
22

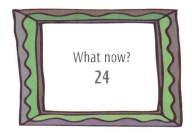
What now?
24

Quiz
26

Projects
29

Your journal
30

Glossary
31

José Luis Morales

ABOUT YOU

Who am I? Good question. Funny that other people think they know me, when I myself don't think I do – at least not completely. I know I am Melinda and Joe's firstborn. I also know that they are not perfect, but they do love me. I know what my little brother and my younger sister say I am (can't say it here, though). I know what my teachers say I am (the shy one in the corner), and my classmates think they know who I am (a geek). But the fact is I am all those things and much more. People say each person is a mix of features they are born with and others they develop according to their experiences and environment. I clearly draw my occasional bad temper from Dad, but where does my preference for black come from? I live in a pretty colorful home, filled with Mom's handmade patchwork quilts and place mats. In fact, nothing in my routine explains my tendency to daydream and understand technologies the way I do. So who am I? I am, for the purpose of this profile, Ayam Mee. Welcome to my life.

How do my brother and my sister see me?

How do my classmates see me?

How do my teachers see me?

How do I see myself?

Nature and nurture

Who am I? Most theories accept that an individual's personality is a combination of genetically determined features ("nature"), and others that are the result of our upbringing combined with our life experiences as we grow up ("nurture"). I think I've inherited my bad temper from Dad's side. But I don't know why I like black. Whatever the reason, I need to learn more about myself to find it out.

You are here to find out.

WHAT ARE YOU LIKE?

Man's fascination with personality, especially with one's genetically inherited features, can be traced back to ancient Greece and Rome. These forerunners of modern scientists have observed four main fluids in the human body: blood, yellow bile, phlegm, and black bile. They believed that having too much or too little of any of these fluids – called "humors" – could make you more or less healthy. It was also believed that a predominance of one of these fluids influenced your personality. Thus, four different types of "temperament" were defined:

Those with a **choleric temperament** (from the Greek word *cholé* for bile, a fluid that helps digestion) were people who got angry easily and were generally aggressive in nature.

People who had a **sanguine temperament** (from the Latin word *sanguis* for blood) were healthy-looking, usually cheerful and well-adjusted, and had lots of friends and admirers.

People with a **phlegmatic temperament** were usually slow, cold, and didn't show much emotion. The word "phlegm" refers to the mucus in our lungs when we have a cold or the flu.

Those with a **melancholic temperament** tended to be sad and pessimistic. The word "melancholy" has become a synonym for sadness, but it comes from the Greek words *melan* (black) and *cholé* (bile). There is no such thing as "black bile" in the human body, so we are not sure what the Greeks meant by that.

Adapted from <http://webspace.ship.edu/cgboer/eysenck.html>.
Accessed on January 26, 2014.

These four temperaments have inspired many theories of personality, including German psychologist Hans Eysenck's, illustrated below.

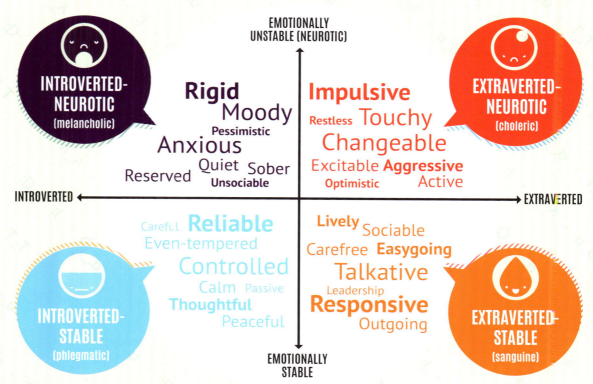

Adapted from <http://tracy-d74.livejournal.com/86221.html>.
Accessed on July 16, 2014.

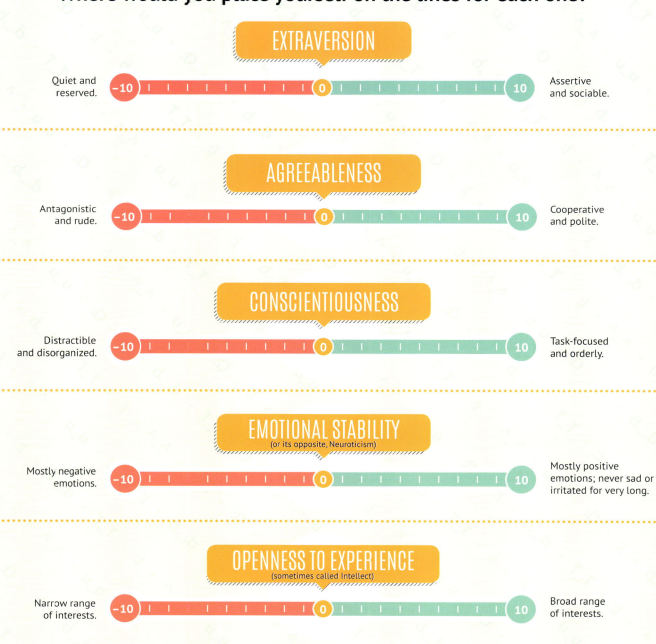

What do you like?

DEFINING TEEN

How do you use your smartphone?

Nowadays, things change so fast we have hardly accustomed ourselves to something we like when it's already out. But in this fast-changing world, one thing seems to remain constant: people like their smartphones and spend lots of time on them. A recent survey attempted to discover what we use them for and for how long every day. The results are shown here. No big surprises in stock for us teenagers, are there? We just love to tap, pinch, and swipe, babe!

Time spent using our smartphones for various activities (minutes per day)

- Browsing the internet — 24
- Checking social networks — 16
- Listening to music — 15
- Playing games — 13
- Making calls — 13
- Text messaging — 11
- Checking/Writing e-mails — 9
- Reading books — 8
- Watching TV/movies — 7
- Taking pictures — 3

Adapted from <http://news.o2.co.uk/?press-release=i-cant-talk-dear-im-on-my-phone>. Accessed on July 28, 2014.

What do teens in the USA spend most of their money on?

Games? Pop concert or movie theater tickets? Do teenagers spend more money on electronics or on clothes and shoes? Businesses really want to know the answers to these questions because they want to have the right products to sell to teens, so they rely on consumer survey experts to get them valuable information. For example, a team at Piper Jaffray, in the USA, conducts an annual survey amongst more than 5,000 American teens to find out what they do with their money. One of the latest surveys shows American teens are spending most of their money on clothes, shoes, and accessories. Yes, you got it. They wanna look good!

Based on <www.piperjaffray.com/2col.aspx?id=287&easeid=1805593>. Accessed on March 7, 2014.

Read the "Taking Stock with Teens" report in full. It's free and loaded with detailed information regarding where teens like to eat, how they consume digital information, and much more.

Access the link <www.piperjaffray.com/2col.aspx?id=287&releaseid=1805593> **and it's all yours.**

Do you identify with their findings? Are there any similarities or differences between how you spend your money and the information below?

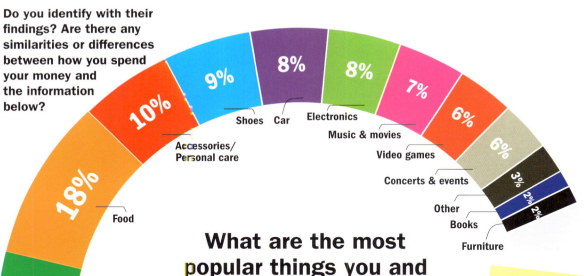

What are the most popular things you and your friends usually spend money on?

That will vary over time

Adapted from <www.marketingpilgrim.com/2013/04/what-are-teens-spending-most-of-their-money-on-surprise-its-not-games.html>. Accessed on February 28, 2014.

WHAT DO YOU NEED?

THINK BEFORE YOU SPEAK

Have you noticed how people use mostly adjectives to talk about other people? Nice, cute, and cool, if you're lucky. Weird, ugly, and fat, if you're me. Then there are those who use nouns to describe (or destroy) you. They come up with phrases like: "an asset to the group" or "the live wire of the classroom". That's if you've done something they liked. More often than I would like, I hear less encouraging phrases describing me as "a disappointment" or "an embarrassment". If people have something to say about me, I wish they used verbs. Then they'd say things like: "She works hard." or "She shows respect." Unfortunately, verbs can be used to be hurtful too: "She dresses like a clown." I know I've heard that. Don't people think before they speak? I don't think so. Everyone needs to feel appreciated, respected, and loved for what they are. Come on, people! How about using **positive** adjectives, noun phrases, and verbs to refer to your fellow humans?

Karen, 14

FROM "UNTEACHABLE" TO "UNBEATABLE":
THE STORY OF ERIN GRUWELL AND HER STUDENTS

A racially diverse group of 150 teenage students considered "unteachable and at risk" graduated from high school. Teacher and students published their story in *The New York Times'* best-selling book *The Freedom Writers Diary,* which later inspired the movie *Freedom Writers*, starring Hilary Swank as Erin Gruwell. This charismatic teacher showed these kids she truly cared by giving them warmth, acceptance, and respect at the same time as she challenged them to set themselves life goals. These kids came from rough neighborhoods in Los Angeles, where gun shootings and drugs were common. As they entered high school, the kids declared they had no interest in learning and that they hated school. Erin responded by inviting them to write a personal journal. The students then discovered they could write and that others were interested in what they had to say. Positive regard allowed them to have dreams. With the help of their teacher, they removed the obstacles that separated them from those dreams. Positive regard, an unbeatable formula for self-actualization!

Based on <www.freedomwritersfoundation.org/about.html>. Accessed on February 28, 2014.

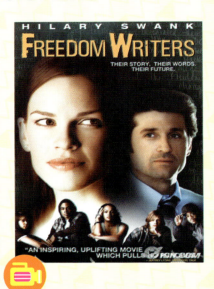

Watch the movie trailer at: <www.youtube.com/watch?v=JhXMJlm852A>.

You can read the whole story at: <www.freedomwritersfoundation.org>.

WHAT WE NEED | POSITIVE REGARD

Humanistic psychologist Carl Rogers believes that **positive regard** is essential for the healthy development of one's self and for successful interpersonal relationships.

Positive regard includes love, sympathy, warmth, acceptance, and respect from our family, friends, and people who are important to us.

Adapted from *Introduction to Psychology*, by R. Plotnik, H. Kouyoumdjian. Singapore: Cengage Learning, 2013. p. 445-446.

PROBABLY LOVE, ACCEPTANCE, AND RESPECT.

HOW DO YOU LEARN BEST?

I love grades, prizes, and trophies!

Tell me what I have to do and I'll do my best. That's all.

I want to do as little as possible.

I prefer to work on my own.

I love working in groups.

Theresa A. Thorkildsen, an American educational psychologist, believes young people have three main sets of needs: the need to feel that they are good at something (competence); the need to relate positively to their family, teachers, and peers (affiliation); and the need of freedom of choice (self-determination). Our family, our school, and our peers expect us to be and to do things in a certain way. It's not always easy to balance what we need with what others expect from us. Thorkildsen has identified seven possible attitudes or orientations at school. Which one(s) best describe(s) YOURS?

Competence   Affiliation   Self-determination

Based on *Motivation and the Struggle to Learn*: Responding to Fractured Experience, by Theresa A. Thorkildsen, John G. Nicholls. Boston: Allyn & Bacon, 2002. p. 13.

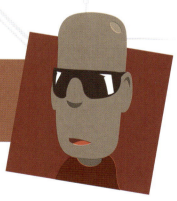

I like to know I can solve problems on my own.

I want to do the work really well, to the last detail.

UNDERSTANDING IT
HELPS YOU DO BETTER.

How do you cope with difficulties?

"Courage is resistance to fear, mastery of fear, not absence of fear."
MARK TWAIN [1]

"The greatest glory in living lies not in never falling, but in rising every time we fall."
NELSON MANDELA [2]

"The thing that is really hard, and really amazing, is giving up on being perfect and beginning the work of becoming yourself."
ANNA QUINDLEN, AMERICAN WRITER AND JOURNALIST [3]

[1] Extracted from <www.brainyquote.com/quotes/quotes/m/marktwain138540.html>. Accessed on February 28, 2014.
[2] Extracted from <www.goodreads.com/quotes/122796-the-greatest-glory-in-living-lies-not-in-never-falling>. Accessed on February 28, 2014.
[3] Extracted from <www.brainyquote.com/quotes/quotes/a/annaquindl390536.html>. Accessed on February 28, 2014.

re·sil·ience
\ri-ˈzil-yən(t)s\

The ability to become strong, healthy, or successful again after something bad happens; the ability of something to return to its original shape after it has been pulled, stretched, pressed, bent, etc.

Extracted from <www.merriam-webster.com/dictionary/resilience>. Accessed on February 28, 2014.

[...] Being resilient doesn't mean going through life without experiencing stress and pain. People feel grief, sadness, and a range of other emotions after adversity and loss. The road to resilience lies in working through the emotions and the effects of stress and painful events. Resilience is not something that you're either born with or without. Resilience develops as people grow up and gain better thinking and self-management skills. Resilience also comes from supportive relationships with parents, peers, and others, as well as cultural beliefs and traditions that help people cope with the inevitable bumps in life. Resilience is found in a variety of behaviors, thoughts, and actions that can be learned and developed throughout your lifetime. [...]

Adapted from <www.pbs.org/thisemotionallife/topic/resilience/what-resilience>. Accessed on February 28, 2014.

Factors that contribute to resilience

- Close relationship with family and friends.
- A positive view of oneself and confidence in one's own strengths and abilities.
- The ability to manage strong feelings and impulses.
- Good problem-solving and communication skills.
- Feeling in control.
- Seeking help and resources.
- Seeing oneself as resilient (rather than as a victim).
- Coping with stress in healthy ways and avoiding harmful coping strategies, such as substance abuse.
- Helping others.
- Finding positive meaning in life despite difficult or traumatic events.

Adapted from <www.pbs.org/thisemotionallife/topic/resilience/what-resilience>. Accessed on February 28, 2014.

First, make sure you understand the problem. Then, plan to solve it in steps.

HOW DO YOU FEEL ABOUT YOUR LOOKS?

I WISH MY BODY LOOKED MORE LIKE THE BODIES I SEE ON TV AND IN MAGAZINES.

THE WESTERN CULTURE'S IDEA THAT A WOMAN MUST BE THIN TO BE BEAUTIFUL IS CALLED **THE THIN IDEAL**. THE OBSESSION WITH THIS IDEAL PLACES ENORMOUS PRESSURE ON WOMEN TO STAY THIN AND YOUNG.

"This ideal stresses slimness, youth and androgyny, rather than the normative female body. The thin-ideal woman portrayed in the media is biogenetically difficult, if not impossible, for the majority of women."

Extracted from "The impact of exposure to the thin-ideal media image on women", by N. Hawkins et al. *Eating Disorders*, v. 12, issue 1, 2004. p. 35-50.

Figures released on www.betterhealth.vic.gov.au reveal:

Approximately 17% of men are dieting at any given time; one in ten people with anorexia are male; 4% of men purge after eating; 3% binge eat; and an estimated 3% of adolescent boys use muscle-enhancing drugs (including steroids) to help achieve the "ideal" body.

→ Adapted from <www.psychology.org.au/publications/inpsych/body_image>. Accessed on February 4, 2014.

"In the past decade or so, we've seen the fastest increase in rates of eating disorders is in adolescent males," said Sari Fine Shepphird, a clinical psychologist and eating disorder expert based in Calabasas, California, USA.

"We've always had fashion magazines that depict an ideal body weight for women, but just over a decade ago, there were very few magazines that appealed an ideal body shape for men," Shepphird said. "Now, there are more than twenty where we have the male body ideal being portrayed."

"Advertisements, models, and actors stress the importance of muscularity to masculinity," Shepphird said.

"Men who are more likely to associate masculinity with big muscles are more likely to engage in behaviors that are unhealthy, like excessive exercise or taking unhealthy supplements to decrease body fat," she said.

→ Adapted from <www.usatoday.com/story/news/health/2013/11/12/eating-disorders-men-increases/3509399/>. Accessed on February 4, 2014.

OK. BUT YOU ARE MUCH MORE THAN YOUR LOOKS.

WHAT MAKES A PERSON ATTRACTIVE, AFTER ALL?

A HISTORY OF HOW BEING "THIN" BECAME A SYNONYM OF BEING "BEAUTIFUL".

Miranda Kerr

The trend of being thin continues to the present day.

2000s

Throughout history, and in different cultures, standards of beauty have differed depending on what is aesthetically pleasing for the time. Frequently, it has been a person's body that has been used as a measure of attractiveness.

Curvy women were considered beautiful. Thinness was associated with sickness and poverty.

Up to the mid-19th century

Based on *Thin Is In: An Analysis of Media Endorsed Ideals of Physical Attractiveness and Their Effects on College-Aged Women*, by Ximena A. Ramirez. Boston College. May 2007.

Do you feel valued and accepted?

What is bullying?
Bullying involves an individual or a group repeatedly harming another person – physically (e.g. punching or pushing), verbally (e.g. teasing or name-calling), or socially (e.g. ostracizing or spreading hurtful rumors). [...]

Most common forms of bullying
[...] According to the U.S. Department of Justice, bullying behavior might include assault, tripping, intimidation, rumor spreading and isolation, demands for money, destruction of property, theft of valued possessions, destruction of another's work, and name-calling. [...] Bullies are able to maintain a more persistent presence in the lives of their victims through cyber-bullying. Researchers define cyber-bullying as "willful and repeated harm inflicted through the use of computers, cell phones and other electronic devices." [...]

Extracted from <www.thebullyproject.com/tools_and_resources>. Accessed on March 7, 2014.

Both the bullied and the bullies need counseling and support — but it should be clear that bullying is wrong and there should be consequences for those who do it.

Celebrities who were bullied

Chris Colfer Colfer was homeschooled for most of middle school because the bullying was so bad. "I was very tiny, [...] I spent most of my time stuffed into lockers. Thank God for cell phones, or I'd still be in there." He says he wasn't honest with himself in high school because the constant bullying convinced him he "couldn't get lower" than being gay.

Adapted from <http://popwatch.ew.com/2011/10/03/chris-colfer-glee-new-yorker-festival/>. Accessed on February 28, 2014.

Jessica Alba "I was bullied really badly at school. My dad had to walk me there so I didn't get attacked. I'd eat my lunch in the nurse's office so I didn't have to sit with the other girls. [...] Apart from my being of mixed race, my parents didn't have money, so I never had the cute clothes or the cool backpack. [...] I feel so bad for any kid who is getting bullied. I've been there. I know how much it hurts and I know how it affects you."

Adapted from <www.dailymail.co.uk/home/moslive/article-489884/Jessica-Alba-Id-definitely-shy-nerdy-type-guy.html>. Accessed on February 28, 2014.

"I believe that every human being on the planet comes with the inherent divine right to be himself and herself."

Oprah Winfrey

Speech given at the launch of Lady Gaga's Born This Way Foundation, Harvard University, on February 29, 2012.

What Makes You Unique?

10 Things that Make You Unique

You are one of a kind. With your lights and your shadows, for better or for worse, you journey through life in a way that is special and unique. Knowing the things that make you who **YOU** are may help you understand how you choose to live your life. Here's a list of 10 of those things.

10
Your beliefs and culture.
What do you think about the mysteries of life and the universe? What you think about spirituality makes you special. What is your culture? How does spirituality manifest itself in your culture? Do you follow these traditions?

9
Your aspirations and goals.
Every day we set goals for ourselves, which might be big or small things we want to achieve. We may or may not be able to complete them, but they are part of what makes us who we are. What do you want to achieve this week, month, year, or in a few years' time?

8
Your relationships.
We are all known especially for how we behave with others. This makes us special, loved, or hated. How do you choose to relate to your family, friends, and the people around you?

1

Your "signature style".
Are you funny, quiet, entertaining, enthusiastic, curious, sweet, adventurous, or calm? What's the first thing that comes to people's minds when they think of you? That's your "signature style". It makes you special. It makes you "YOU".

2

Your past experiences.
Everyone has had both good and bad experiences in the past. These experiences and the unique things we learn from them mold our character and make us different from everyone else.

3

Ethics and morals instilled in you.
Every decision you make in life will be guided by the ethics and morals you have learned at home, at school, in your social interactions, in your society, and in your culture. The way you interpret social norms will be evident in everything you do.

4

Attitude.
Attitude can either make or ruin you. People will remember you for your attitude towards them and towards life. Do you mostly have a positive or a negative attitude?

5

Your appearance says a lot about you.
Your hair, your style, your accessories, your make-up, and your confidence. Your appearance plays an important role in building up your individuality. It is all about how you present yourself to the world.

7

Your habits and hobbies.
Are you a computer geek or a bookworm? Do you follow fashion? Are you an athlete or an artist? What you do every day and your interests make you the way you are.

6

Your way of communicating.
How do you communicate with the people around you? Your accent, your language, your expressions, your texts, your writings, and your gestures are an important part of your personality.

YOU ARE YOU AND NO ONE ELSE.

Based on <http://listdose.com/10-things-that-make-you-unique>. Accessed on February 17, 2014.

WHAT *now*?

The greatest adventure is what lies ahead.
Today and tomorrow are yet to be said.
The chances, the changes are all yours to make.
The mold of your life is in your hands to break.

J.R.R. Tolkien, *The Hobbit*
(song "The Greatest Adventure", by Jules Bass)

Extracted from <www.jjjwebdevelopment.com/306sites/hobbitsong/hobbitsong.shtml>. Accessed on February 28, 2014.

THE PRESENT IS THE FOOD OF THE FUTURE.

Edward Counsel, *Maxims*

Extracted from <www.notable-quotes.com/p/present_quotes.html>. Accessed on July 28, 2014.

SUCCESS ISN'T PERMANENT, and FAILURE ISN'T FATAL.

MIKE DITKA

Extracted from <www.quotationspage.com/quote/31660.html/>. Accessed on May 6, 2014.

THE BEST WAY to predict your future is TO CREATE IT.

ABRAHAM LINCOLN

Extracted from <www.goodreads.com/quotes/328848-the-best-way-to-predict-your-future-is-to-create>. Accessed on July 28, 2014.

Difficult to see. ALWAYS IN MOTION IS THE FUTURE.

YODA, STAR WARS
EPISODE V: THE EMPIRE STRIKES BACK

Extracted from <www.destinationhollywood.com/movies/starwars/moviequotes_yoda.shtml>. Accessed on July 28, 2014.

Success is liking **yourself**, liking **what you do**, and liking **how you do it**.

MAYA ANGELOU

Extracted from <https://fbcdn-sphotos-f-a.akamaihd.net/hphotos-ak-frc3/t1/307910_10151423678764171_117971221_n.jpg>. Accessed on February 17, 2014.

Love not what you are,
but what you may become.

Miguel de Cervantes

Extracted from <www.quotes.net/authors/miguel+de+cervantes>. Accessed on May 30, 2014.

There is now no smooth road into the future: but we go round, or scramble over the obstacles.

D. H. Lawrence

Extracted from <http://classiclit.about.com/od/ladychatterleyslover/a/Lady-Chatterleys-Lover-Quotes.htm>. Accessed on July 28, 2014.

KEEP LEARNING. KEEP DREAMING. KEEP GOING! *never give up!*

QUIZ

◆ **PAGES 2 TO 5**
CHECK (✓) THE CORRECT ANSWER.

1 Joe and Melinda are
  a ☐ Ayam's brother and sister.
  b ☐ Ayam's parents.

2 How many brothers and sisters does Ayam mention in his profile?
  a ☐ Two.
  b ☐ Three.

3 Ayam really appreciates
  a ☐ technology.
  b ☐ patchwork.

4 Who likes to dress in black?
  a ☐ Ayam's mother does.
  b ☐ Ayam does.

5 Who has an occasional bad temper?
  a ☐ Ayam and his mother do.
  b ☐ Ayam and his father do.

6 "Nurture" refers to
  a ☐ the part of our personality we are born with.
  b ☐ the part of our personality we develop as we grow up.

7 People who had a sanguine temperament were
  a ☐ healthy-looking, usually cheerful, and well-adjusted.
  b ☐ angry and aggressive.

8 If you are open to experience, it means
  a ☐ you are not interested in knowing what is new.
  b ☐ you have a broad range of interests.

◆ **PAGES 6 TO 9**
CHECK (✓) THE CORRECT ANSWER.

1 It is difficult to answer the question "What do teenagers like?" because
  a ☐ what teens like never changes.
  b ☐ what teens like generally changes rapidly.

2 What do people spend most time doing on their smartphones?
  a ☐ Browsing the internet.
  b ☐ Checking social networks.

3 How many minutes do people spend playing games on their smartphones?
  a ☐ Fifteen minutes.
  b ☐ Thirteen minutes.

4 According to the text on page 7, which item do teenagers spend most of their money on?
  a ☐ Electronics.
  b ☐ Clothing.

5 A survey carried out by a team at Piper Jaffray was conducted with
  a ☐ more than 5,000 American teens.
  b ☐ less than 5,000 American teens.

6 What percentage of their money do American teens spend on music and movies?
  a ☐ 6%
  b ☐ 7%

7 Why were the teenagers portrayed on the movie *Freedom Writers* considered "unteachable and at risk"?
  a ☐ Because they had positive regard.
  b ☐ Because they came from rough neighborhoods.
  c ☐ Because they had many dreams.

8 What did Erin Gruwell do to motivate her students?
  a ☐ She declared she had no interest in teaching.
  b ☐ She invited her students to make a movie and write a book.
  c ☐ She showed the kids she truly cared by giving them warmth, acceptance, and respect.

ASSIGNMENT
Conduct a survey in your class to find out how your classmates use their smartphones. Design the questions and ask them around. Then, collect the data and make a bar graph (horizontal or vertical). Put together a short slide presentation to share your results with the group.

◆ **PAGES 10 TO 17**
UNSCRAMBLE THE LETTERS TO FORM THE THREE MAIN SETS OF NEEDS YOUNG PEOPLE HAVE.

1 ☐☐☐☐☐☐☐☐☐
N C M E T E C E O P

2 ☐☐☐☐☐☐☐☐☐☐
A I L I F I O N F A T

3 ☐☐☐☐-☐☐☐☐☐☐☐☐☐☐☐
E S L F R E T E M I A T I O N D N

26

CIRCLE THE CORRECT ANSWER.

1 Resilience is
  a the ability to quit when you feel something is difficult.
  b the ability to give up before trying hard.
  c the ability to become strong, healthy, or successful again after something bad happens.

2 According to research released on an Australian website,
  a approximately 17% of men are dieting.
  b 30% of male teens take drugs to build up muscles.
  c one in five people with anorexia are men.

3 When was the first Barbie doll launched?
  a In 1960. **b** In 1917. **c** In 1959.

4 Who was Twiggy?
  a A famous fashion designer.
  b A famous thin model of the 1960s.
  c A famous model who died young.

ASSIGNMENT
Have you suffered and/or witnessed any kind of bullying at school? Write a brief account of what happened one of those times, how you felt, and what you did. Record your account on <http://vocaroo.com> and share it with your teacher or another adult you trust. Request that it be confidential.

COMPLETE THE SENTENCES BELOW WITH 6 WORDS FROM THE BOX.

UNBEATABLE ANOREXIA STRESS TREND UNTEACHABLE PRIORITIZE ATTITUDE CHOLERIC

1 If you get irritated easily and lose your patience, your temperament is _____.

2 Someone who is confrontational and fights a lot has a bad _____.

3 Sue is under a lot of _____ because her mid-term exams are coming up.

4 To _____ means to organize things according to how important they are.

5 _____ is an eating disorder that makes people stop eating.

6 The _____ of being thin started many years ago.

27

FIND THE WORDS THAT ANSWER THE QUESTIONS BELOW AND BREAK THE CODE.

1 What did psychologist Carl Rogers say everyone needed?

1	2	4	5	6	5	7	8	*	9	8	10	11	9	12

2 Which expression does Sue use to indicate her mid-term exams are about to take place?

20	2	14	5	19	10	*	16	1

3 What's the word for repeatedly harming someone physically, verbally, or socially?

15	16	17	17	18	5	19	10

4 How do you call people who just watch instead of helping when someone is being bullied?

15	18	4	6	11	19	12	8	9

5 What does Sue's mother say to show she trusts her daughter?

5	*	21	19	2	3	*	18	2	16	*	20	11	19	*	12	2	*	5	6

6 What do you call the ability humans have to recover after something bad happens to them?

9	8	4	5	17	5	8	19	20	8

7 One word for saying in the future.

11	13	8	11	12

FILL OUT THE DIAGRAM WITH THE NUMBERED LETTERS FROM THE ACTIVITY ABOVE AND FIND THE MYSTERY QUOTE.

| 5 | 6 | | 12 | 2 | 8 | 4 | | 19 | 2 | 6 | | 14 | 11 | 6 | 6 | 8 | 9 |

| 13 | 2 | 3 | | 4 | 17 | 2 | 3 | 17 | 18 | | 18 | 2 | 16 | | 10 | 2 |

| 11 | 4 | | 17 | 2 | 19 | 10 | | 11 | 4 | | 18 | 2 | 16 | | 12 | 2 |

| 19 | 2 | 6 | | 4 | 6 | 2 | 1 |

28

PROJECTS

YOU ARE JOINING A NEW SOCIAL NETWORK

Make a two-minute personal movie to be displayed in your profile on a social network. In the scenes, use text and pictures that do not show people, just symbols that represent your personality and important moments in your life, from the day you were born until today. Choose your own background music.

→ I am...
→ I was born on...
→ At school...
→ A great birthday party.
→ A fun moment with my family.
→ A fun moment with my friends.
→ My adventures in...
→ My passion(s).
→ High school snapshots.
→ What now?

FIND A POPULAR ONLINE PERSONALITY TEST

Take the test and then exchange links with a classmate. Share the results with each other and your teacher. Do you all agree?

FIND A POPULAR ONLINE EMOTIONAL RESILIENCE TEST

Take the test and exchange links with a classmate. Then share the results with each other and your teacher. Do you all agree?

YOU ARE APPLYING FOR A COURSE

As part of the process, you are asked to record yourself explaining what you and those who know you think your "signature style" is. You can do it with your smartphone.

YOU ARE PRESIDENT OF THE SENIOR GRADUATING CLASS

You want to start an awareness raising campaign against bullying in your school. Make a list of action points for the year.

YOU ARE A JOURNALIST

Use the results of the class survey about the use of smartphones to post a description of it on a blog, as well as your predictions about their use in the near future.

YOU ARE YOURSELF

Use Ayam Mee's profile on pages 2-3 as a model to write your own on a social network.

YOU ARE YOUR OWN MOM OR DAD

Write an e-mail you imagine your parents would send you when things are not OK for you. You can refer to the story on pages 18-19.

YOU ARE A TROUBLED TEENAGER

Write a dialogue you can have with your parents so that they understand you need help. Use the story on pages 18-19 as a reference.

29

YOUR JOURNAL.
YOUR THOUGHTS AND IDEAS.

- WHO ARE YOU?

- WHAT ARE YOU LIKE?

- WHAT DO YOU LIKE?

- WHAT DO YOU NEED?

- HOW DO YOU LEARN BEST?

- HOW DO YOU COPE WITH DIFFICULTIES?

- HOW DO YOU FEEL ABOUT YOUR LOOKS?

- WHAT MAKES A PERSON ATTRACTIVE, AFTER ALL?

- DO YOU AND YOUR PARENTS LISTEN TO ONE ANOTHER?

- DO YOU FEEL VALUED AND ACCEPTED?

- WHAT MAKES YOU UNIQUE?

- WHAT NOW?

GLOSSARY

A
achieve reach, obtain, succeed
agreeable pleasant
assertive behaves in a confident way
asset something valuable
avoiding preventing something from happening

B
binge eat eat too much, too quickly
bookworm someone who reads a lot
breakdown a sudden health problem, a mental condition in which a person is so upset or unhappy that he/she cannot look after him/herself

C
carefree easygoing, happy, and having no worries
cliche a phrase used so often it's not original
conscientious responsible, diligent, and careful
curvy with curves

D
daydream have happy thoughts, spend time thinking about something pleasant
decrease reduce
deserves be worthy of

E
embarrassed made someone feel ashamed
engage become involved

F
fit in belong, to be accepted
forerunners those who came before, precursors

G
geek a person who is very interested in or even obsessed with an intellectual hobby or pastime, very often related to technology
grab hold
grief a strong feeling of sadness

H
harming causing damage
hurt cause someone physical or emotional pain

I
inherited be born with, receive from an ancestor
instilled taught gradually

J
journey travel

L
live wire lively and energetic

M
manage handle, deal successfully with a problem or a difficult situation
mid-term in the middle of the school term
moody constantly changing moods, likely to become unhappy or angry for no particular reason

N
narrow not wide, limited in range or variety

O
ostracizing excluding from the group
outgoing friendly, someone who enjoys meeting and talking to people

P
poverty the state of being poor
purge eliminate food after eating

Q
quiet people who do not usually speak a lot
quilts bed covers

R
restless nervous
rough dangerous

S
seeking looking for
shootings fights with firearms
sickness illness
skyrocketed increased very quickly and suddenly
slenderness thinness
slimness slenderness, thinness
sober with a serious attitude
struggling having difficulties
survey a set of questions asked to a large number of people
sympathy caring about someone's suffering, showing support

T
teasing making fun of, laughing, and criticizing
temper tendency to be angry
threatened vulnerable, menaced
touchy easily upset, oversensitive
tripping making someone fall

U
ugly not beautiful
unbeatable excellent, impossible to defeat
upbringing care and teaching received during childhood
upset unhappy, anxious, or annoyed

W
weird strange
willful obstinate
wish want something to happen

Direção: Sandra Possas
Edição executiva de inglês: Izaura Valverde
Gerência de produção: Christiane Borin
Edição executiva de conteúdos digitais: Adriana Pedro de Almeida
Coordenação de arte: Raquel Buim

Edição: Cristina Cesar, Henrique Zanardi
Assistência editorial: Bruna Marini, Nathália Horvath
Revisão: Giuliana Gramani, Rafael Gustavo Spigel, Raymond Shoulder, Roberta Moratto Risther, Sheila Saad, Vivian Cristina de Souza
Projeto gráfico: Hulda Melo
Edição de arte: Hulda Melo
Capa: Raquel Buim, sob ilustração de Tsha/Shutterstock
Criações: Amanda Miyuki de Sá, Carol Cavaleiro, Iansã Negrão, Ilustre BOB, Inara Negrão, Ivan Luiz, Olavo Costa
Iconografia: Yan Imagens
Tratamento de imagens: Arleth Rodrigues, Bureau São Paulo, Marina M. Buzzinaro, Resolução Arte e Imagem
Pré-impressão: Alexandre Petreca, Everton L. de Oliveira Silva, Fabio N. Precendo, Hélio P. de Souza Filho, Marcio H. Kamoto, Rubens M. Rodrigues, Vitória Sousa
Impressão e acabamento: Yan Imagens
Lote: 749373

Créditos das fotos

p. 2: ©Thinkstock/Getty Images; p. 3: ©Thinkstock/Getty Images, ©NiraMalyna/Shutterstock, ©Thinkstock/Getty Images, ©Thinkstock/Getty Images; p. 6: ©Thinkstock/Getty Images; p. 9: Reprodução; p. 12: ©FPG/Equipa/Archive Photos/Getty Images, ©Thinkstock/Getty Images, ©Bobby Bank/WireImage/Getty Images; p. 14: Reprodução, ©Edyta Pawlowska/Shutterstock; p. 15: Reprodução; p. 16: ©Thinkstock/Getty Images, ©Featureflash/Shutterstock, ©Franz Xavier Winterhalter/The Bridgeman Art Library/Getty Images, ©Victorian Traditions/Shutterstock; p. 17: ©UPPA/Diomedia, ©Express Newspapers/Freelancer/Hulton Archive/Getty Images, ©Barry Lewis/Latinstock, ©DIOMEDIA/Photononstop/SCREEN, ©Latinstock/GraphicaArtis/Corbis, ©H. Armstrong Roberts/Retrofile/Getty Images, ©The Beauty Redefined Foundation, ©The Beauty Redefined Foundation, ©The Beauty Redefined Foundation; p. 21: ©Featureflash/Shutterstock, Thinkstock/Getty Images.

Todos os *sites* mencionados nesta obra foram reproduzidos apenas para fins didáticos. A Richmond não tem controle sobre seu conteúdo, o qual foi cuidadosamente verificado antes de sua utilização.

Embora todas as medidas tenham sido tomadas para identificar e contatar os detentores de direitos autorais sobre os materiais reproduzidos nesta obra, isso nem sempre foi possível. A editora estará pronta a retificar quaisquer erros dessa natureza assim que notificada.

Websites mentioned in this material were quoted for didactic purposes only. Richmond has no control over their content and urges care when using them.

Every effort has been made to trace the copyright holders, but if any omission can be rectified, the publishers will be pleased to make the necessary arrangements.

Dados Internacionais de Catalogação na Publicação (CIP)
(Câmara Brasileira do Livro, SP, Brasil)

Morales, José Luis
    Learn about identity / José Luis Morales. —
São Paulo : Moderna, 2014.

    1. Inglês — Estudo e ensino I. Título.

14-04494   CDD-420.7

Índices para catálogo sistemático:
1. Inglês : Estudo e ensino 420.7

ISBN 978-85-16-09523-9

Reprodução proibida. Art. 184 do Código Penal e Lei 9.610, de 19 de fevereiro de 1998.
Todos os direitos reservados.

©Editora Moderna Ltda.

RICHMOND
EDITORA MODERNA LTDA.
Rua Padre Adelino, 758 – Belenzinho
São Paulo – SP – Brasil – CEP 03303-904
www.richmond.com.br
2022
Impresso no Brasil